Passive Income

The Ultimate High Yielding Income Strategy

Cedric Nix

from various sources. Please consult a licensed professional before attempting any techniques outlined in this book.

By reading this document, the reader agrees that under no circumstances are is the author responsible for any losses, direct or indirect, which are incurred as a result of the use of information contained within this document, including, but not limited to, —errors, omissions, or inaccuracies.

Table of Contents

Introduction

"Take responsibility for your finances—or get used to taking orders for the rest of your life. You're either a master of money or a slave to it. Your choice." – Robert T. Kiyosaki

I want to thank you for choosing this book, "Passive Income: The Ultimate High Yielding Income Strategy" and I sincerely hope you find it useful.

This book is my way of giving back to the community by sharing my knowledge and experience with you that I have acquired over the years. You see, I have been very fortunate in my life in some ways. I have had many mentors throughout my life who have taught me how to build real wealth.

I've worked in a variety of sectors and industries, and I have also started many business ventures. Some of them failed and many of them were super successful, which is why I am now free from ever working again in my life. But the most important thing is what all the businesses – both the failed ones and the successful ones – taught me over all these years.

So in this book, I am going to share with you the secrets of building real wealth. And when I talk about real wealth, I mean more than just money. Building genuine wealth is as much about building a source of income as it is about building the person. So let's get started with this book.

I hope you like it and I hope it helps you reach your goal of getting financial freedom by way of generating passive income. Good luck and let's get started!

Chapter 1:

The Rat Race

The world is a completely different place now from what it used to be a couple decades ago. The times have changed, and not exactly for the better, I'm afraid. America has fallen off gold standard already, and we've had our fair share of economic crises. And whenever these recessions have happened, we've had a steady flow of panic inducing headlines, locker room talk, and foreclosures. Wall street fiascos and Ponzi schemes are now a common thing, and there's just a whole bunch of bad news all around. Sure, we might be in recovery right now, but that doesn't mean it can't and won't happen again. Gainful employment has been declining and unemployment is on the rise. It is affecting everyone from bankers to managers to blue-collar workers.

You might think that all that bad news must've taught people to know better than to depend on their "safe and secure" jobs, but they still do. Job security is a relic of the past, people, and those who don't realize it are in for a huge shock. And if you think

Social Security will take care of you, you've got another thing coming.

And yet, even the people who already realize this don't try to find a secondary source of income for themselves. It's like they actually *like* trading their time for money and don't wish to have financial liberty at all. It's shocking, I know.

"Those who don't learn from history are doomed to repeat it."

And that's exactly what we've been doing. We've done this over and over again and yet we still don't learn from our mistakes. Because of our educational institutions failing to provide an adequate knowledge of the working of finance and economy, people keep making bad decisions and falling into the same traps over and over. The 2009 economic crash happened because people fell back into their old habits and a sense of complacency plagued the nation. We used our homes as ATMs and cash cows, liquid money was losing money real quick, and it all had to end eventually. The fantasy had to come crashing down at some point, and when it did, millions of people lost their 401Ks.

Right now, we're living in difficult times. There's a huge increase in the number of people without homes, the number of people living below the poverty line, and the number of people who don't have enough to retire with ease. A lot of bad news, huh? So I guess I finally have your attention. Good, this means that you won't be hitting the snooze button tomorrow. You will actually be waking up on time and make yourself that cup of coffee so you can feel ready to hustle.

The only way for you to actually secure your future is to take control of it yourself. Your stocks won't help you and the same goes for your mutual funds. They're neither smart nor secure. You need to be smarter and invest in something much more secure.

The Current Economy

So let's talk about the Information Age, shall we?

You must remember how your parents always told you that there is only one formula to success: Study hard >> Get good grades >> Get a secure, high-paying job >> You are now successful.

Remember that? Yeah, that may have worked during your parents' time, but it doesn't work anymore. It's 20th century thinking, and it isn't becoming of someone who wants to live in the now. We're not in the Industrial Age anymore. This is the Information Age, so if you want to make the best of your life right now, you need to update yourself on how the world works currently.

The old rules don't apply anymore. Nobody will take care of you if you fall – not the government, not your job, not your friends, nobody will. The only person who can do that is you. Job security, pension plans, and retirement funds are a thing of the past, so you can't rely on them.

And for that to happen, you need to realize the existence of the rat race that our society has been pushing everyone into for so many years now. The Success Formula your parents relied on so much has been making people climb the corporate ladder without ever stopping to observe what's happening around them. People spend their entire lives looking at the behind of the person above them, wishing to move up and take their place eventually. Is that how you want to spend your whole life? I don't think so.

So what are you going to do about it? Blaming the government won't help, blaming the system won't help; blaming the people around you will definitely won't help. The only thing that *will* help is taking control of your life and your finances.

Escape the Rat Race

Employment is not as "normal" as one would think, historically speaking. It's actually something that is fairly recent. In Agrarian times, basically everyone was a businessman. People used the king's lands and paid some tax to the state in return.

Passive Income

Farmers, butchers, blacksmiths, bakers – they didn't make their living by being employees.

This concept of employment came from Prussia, where the president decided to provide retirement plans to people after the age of 65. This wasn't a problem for them since the average life expectancy of people there during the 1890s was about 45 years. Their government wanted to mass-produce employees and soldiers, and that's exactly what they did.

Now that people's average life expectancies have almost doubled, this is no longer a viable system. And yet people continue to believe in the security of regular jobs and retirement funds. We've been brainwashed into believing in this system to bad that we won't get ourselves out of it no matter how much evidence we see that points to its failures.

But I see hope, because people are slowly but steadily realizing that this is a faulty system. Each economic crisis brings them that much closer to realizing that the corporate security is a myth and they need to create their wealth by their own means. People are waking up to the fact that employment is a very limited way of generating income and they need to broaden their horizons if they want a better life. And the way to do it is entrepreneurship.

The time is ripe for you to take advantage of all this potential that the current economy is offering, and **escape the rat race for good**.

Chapter 2:

Taking The Reins

So now that you've decided to get out of the rat race that has plagued the world, it's time to think about how you want to go about achieving that. It's all about your mindset. If you can't create the right mindset, you won't be able to achieve anything, and this applies to everything you do in life, not just setting up a business.

Think about how many entrepreneurs have started out completely broke and lived in suboptimal conditions for long periods of time before they got their big break and finally "made it" as we call it. There are far too many, and the only reason they were able to achieve what they did was because they had the right mindset, and they stuck to it in their toughest times.

I remember how Phil, one of my fellow business partners in one of our ventures, started out. Back in 1990, all he and his wife had was a small amount of savings and an old car. They had both left their jobs to be entrepreneurs and were homeless. He tells me, "It wasn't so bad for the first few weeks, you know. We had our credit cards and a lot of optimism. But after sleeping in the car every single night, exhausting our credit cards, and eating instant noodles for three weeks straight, we began to wrap our heads around what was really happening and the situation we were in."

Needless to say, it was really harsh for them for a few years. They lived in the basement of one of their friends' apartments for a while, doing small, and odd jobs every now and then to feed themselves.

Why am I telling you all this?

It's because when people are in such difficult situations and their loved ones tell them to "just get a job", it becomes very difficult to explain why they don't want to, especially to people who naturally value having a job over everything else. It becomes hard to prevail. But they did, and they did it really well. They did have moments of self-doubt, like everyone does once in a while, but they got through those moments because they knew what they wanted.

And do you know what that was? It was financial freedom.

They were both college graduates possessing the skills and work ethic that could get them handsome jobs, but they weren't looking for job security, no. What they wanted was to get out of the rat race and create true wealth for themselves. They're millionaires now, and it's only because of their perseverance and their mindset.

That is all you need to attain genuine financial freedom. Don't make or let others make excuses like "It takes money to make money" or "You need to have a good formal education to realize such dreams."

Phil and his wife were in debt when they started out, and it took them only about six years to become millionaires. They didn't get any handouts along the way, but they still made it to the other side of the financial abyss they were in. So if you want to be able to do the same, what you really need is not money or good formal education, but rather a concrete dream, a hunger for knowledge, and a whole lot of willpower to persevere.

The Myth of Hard Work

Let me just put it out there before we even touch the subject of making money. Hard work alone won't get you anywhere. Yes, I can hear most of you gasp in disbelief, because that's not what most of us have been brought up to believe. Throughout our lives, we keep hearing that if we just work hard enough, it will be all right, that if we just work hard enough, we will be able to achieve anything we desire. That's complete bull, and the saddest part is that most of us will still continue to believe this even when we see so much evidence around us that points to the opposite of this.

Just look around. Don't you know any people who work really hard throughout their lives and still only manage to live at the subsistence level or below that? There are far too many people like that in the world, so of course you know one of them. They work hard their entire lives and still live in difficulty, and what's even more tragic is that they think it's because of their own shortcomings. They feel like if they had just worked a bit harder, they would've made it. They think that they don't have what it takes to be successful.

That's complete hogwash. You need to get over the hard work myth – yes, a myth – and start doing smart work. You need to think smartly and know what things you can control and what you can't. That's how you get true financial freedom. But smart work doesn't exempt you from doing hard work, let me just say. Nothing exempts you from that and you would be an idiot to believe there's a quick, easy, and/or painless way to become rich. There isn't, and if you believe there is, give my guy a call. I think I have some great credit-default swap offers and subprime mortgages for you.

I'm kidding. But the point is yes, hard work is important and you won't get anywhere without it. But there's *more* to becoming successful than just that. You need to work hard *and* in the right direction. So what direction is that?

"Making money, what else?" That's what you're thinking, I know. But there's a problem with that sort of thinking: you don't make a lot of money by working hard to make a lot of money.

Sounds paradoxical? Sure, but that's how things work in the real world. You've seen people who work from paycheck to paycheck, and many of them work really hard five or six days a week, only to spend all they make and then work hard to make it all again.

What's the solution? How do you get out of the loop? It's simple; you take control. And since you can't control the market or the economy the best thing to take control of is the source of your income. Do that and you're golden.

The Roadblock

So what's stopping you from building a business?

Well, there are a few big reasons that stop most people from ever being able to build a successful business. To understand that, you must first know about the four quadrants people live in. These are:

- Employment

- Self-employment

- Investment

- Business

People in each of these quadrants have very different mindsets and core values, and those are the things that govern their lives. Most of us live in the E quadrant, some of us in the S quadrant, and very few in the 'I and the B' quadrants. The quadrant we live in affects how we think and how we approach life. People who live in the E quadrant enjoy the security of a regular job, while people in the B quadrant may hate it and would rather be looking to build wealth.

Now, the best way to build genuine wealth is to live in the B quadrant, to create a business. There are examples of that all around the world and you don't even have to think very hard to come up with the names of entrepreneurs who are extremely rich. Bill Gates, Michael Dell, Steve Jobs, they all became super rich by building their own businesses. So if you want to build genuine wealth, you need to change your mindset from that of the E quadrant to that on the B quadrant.

But it isn't an easy transition. There are many roadblocks to your entry in the B quadrant, and most people are not well equipped to deal with them. For one, many business ideas require upfront capital to be invested in them before any work can actually start, and most of us just don't have that kind of money lying around. Then there's the presence of risk, the high chance of failure that deters most of us from investing that money in a business even if we have it.

Did you know that 90% of new businesses fail in less than five years of their inception? That's a heartbreaking statistic, and it's part of the reason why so many people are afraid of investing in a business. Heck, even I failed the first time around when I was building a business and I lost over a million dollars.

Even if you are ready to take the risk, there is yet another thing that's stopping you. You will have to sacrifice your lifestyle. This is because in the first few years of the operation of a business, you are not making any profits (most businesses aren't, at least), and yet you have to pay the rent, the overhead, your suppliers, your employees, and other costs on time to make sure the business doesn't shut down. What this means is that *you* don't get paid. You may easily go a few years without drawing an actual salary out of the business, and let me tell you that it isn't fun. Remember Phil and his wife living in their car? Yeah, that's the kind of sacrifice people have to make. It can make people absolutely grumpy and miserable, and the only thing that drives them forward at that point is their resolve.

So you understand now why most people can't move to the B quadrant. It requires a lot of mental and physical fortitude to be able to handle whatever comes your way.

Franchises

So let's talk about franchises. You might be thinking that they're a great way to start doing business without risk, right? Well, yes. That part is true; it does take a lot of risk out of your business idea, especially if the franchise is well established like, say, McDonalds or KFC. With a good business plan, your chances of success are pretty good. But there's still one problem even with a franchise – you still need a lot of upfront capital to invest in the business.

Let's say you want to take a franchise. You will have to pay anywhere from $150,000 to $2 million, maybe even more, just to acquire the rights to that franchise. After that, you will also have to send some commission per month to the headquarters. And that's not all. You will also have to pay for training, support, advertising and much more. You can imagine how much of a hassle this can be.

Even after all of this, you don't get any guarantee of success from this plan. Forget making huge profits, you may even run in loss for a few years, and even if you do succeed, you may not earn as big as you had dreamed of. It's a gamble honestly, and

I'm not one to recommend gambling. One in three franchises fail eventually, and while those odds aren't too bad, they still aren't good enough to invest so much of your hard earned money into. I have personally known multiple people over the years that invested all their life savings into franchises that were considered to be failsafe, only to fail later because of a variety of reasons.

The Faucet

The previous few sections probably sounded a bit too negative to you and I might have even scared you off from the idea of starting up a business at all. But don't worry, that's for the really hardcore people. You won't have to face that kind of problems, at least not to such an extent.

Anyway, coming back to the point let me end this chapter on a positive note by enlightening you about **passive income**. Then, in the following chapters, we can study it in more depth and understand it better.

I shall start off with the example of a spring-loaded faucet. You may have seen one in public restrooms, installed there for the purpose of saving water. As long as you're holding the faucet in the 'on' position, the water will keep flowing, but as soon as you let go, the water flow will also stop. That is how most people's income works. They live from paycheck to paycheck, so as long as they're working and putting in their full effort, they will keep earning, and as soon as they stop, their income will also stop, give or take a few months.

This is no way of living with total financial freedom. To do that, you must create a faucet that keeps giving you money without you having to make full efforts for it all your life. You want to secure a source of income that keeps giving you money not just for a few years but also for the rest of your life. This is what we call passive income. It keeps flowing in long after you've invested the money and effort into creating the source of this income.

If you want to create some nice passive income, the first thing you need to do is obviously shift your mindset from the E quadrant to the B quadrant, i.e. be business-minded. But this is not enough. Only building a business is not the solution, since many businesses require you to keep operating and putting in effort to earn. If you manufacture electronics, you will have to keep doing it for you to keep earning. If you have a restaurant, you will have to keep serving people to keep the income flowing in. That's just how most traditional businesses work.

So what you need is a way to create a business avenue where your effort is not required after a certain extent. And the best way to do this, I have discovered, is through a business model called affiliate marketing.

Passive Income

This model of business requires very little upfront investment to begin, and the overhead costs are also very low. You can start working on it in your free time because it has a very flexible operational leverage. As you start earning more and more through it, you can transition out of your day job. We will talk about this in greater detail in one of the following chapters.

Chapter 3:

Passive Income

I n this chapter, we will dive deeper into the nitty-gritties of what passive income actually is. Let's get started.

What is Passive Income?

Many people have the notion that passive income is that easy money you make while you're sitting at a beach chilling, taking slow sips out of your exotic mojito. While that may not be completely incorrect, passive income does take some effort and monetary investment in most cases, at least in the initial stages. By definition, passive income is any income you generate passively, i.e. income you make without actually investing much active effort into it. So for example, if you have a property and you rent it out to someone, the income you gain from it in the form of rent is passive income. Another example would be earnings that come from limited partnership in stocks.

But if we really study it in detail, passive income doesn't just create itself. You have to do something to create the source first.

To earn money passively, you have to first invest some time, effort, and money into setting up the channel. People often confuse it with windfall gain, which is absolutely not the same thing. Windfall gain is money you get unexpectedly. It isn't planned, and there's no work that has been done to earn it. On the other hand, earning passive income does require you to do a fair bit of planning and investment. In short, you do have to **work for it**, at least in the beginning. Examples of windfall would be winning a lottery or inheriting something from your grandparents. But royalties earned by an artist from his or her work are not windfall. They've worked to create a source for the income in the past, and hence, it is their passive income.

An initial amount of investment is crucial for generating some passive income, regardless of how big or small the amount might be. You put in the money and the effort, and then later, with the passage of some time, money starts to flow in in the form of passive income. Once you've set up the funnel, you don't need to engage yourself any more. You can just sit back and enjoy the regular flow of passive income. The upfront work is done and all that is left is to reap the rewards. It's a secondary source of your income that doesn't require you to keep making efforts. Once you get the ball rolling, the revenues start generating on their own.

Passive Income

The income of an individual can generally be classified into three categories:

- Active income

- Passive income

- Portfolio income

Passive income is that income which is generated from either rental or trade activity. You don't have to participate in it in any way. That is why it is also sometimes called residual income.

Common Misconceptions about Passive Income

Let me clear some misconceptions that people have about passive income.

Passive income is not a one-time lump sum income. Many people think that way, but that's actually not passive income, even if there's no effort involved on your part in acquiring that sum of money. For an income to be called passive, it needs to be regular in nature. If it lacks continuity, it isn't passive income. Getting rent from a property would be called passive income because it has that consistency that is the hallmark of passive income.

Passive income is not permanent. Many people seem to think it is, but that is not the case. It may go on for a really long time, maybe even more than a century, but eventually, it must and it will come to an end. How long it will last generally depends on the initial input and steps taken to amplify it. Patents and copyrights are some of the sources that can generate passive income for a really long time.

Passive income is not failsafe on its own. Yes, I had to say it. The whole point of this book is to teach you not to rely on one source of income, and that also applies even when that lone source of income is passive income. Some people fall into the trap of getting complacent once they start generating good amount of passive income, but you must realize that nothing is foolproof, not even your source of passive income. So don't rely solely on it, unless of course, you have **multiple sources of passive income!**

Passive income doesn't mean unaccountable income! I can't stress this enough. Just because you aren't making any active efforts to generate that income doesn't mean you can bail out of reporting that income to the concerned tax authorities. It *is* your income and you *do* have to pay taxes on it to the government.

Chapter 4:

Affiliate Marketing - What is it?

Affiliate marketing is all about a relationship between the advertiser, network, publisher and consumer. It is a talent-based marketing where you get rewarded whenever you bring a customer in. Out of the four major players in affiliate marketing, the advertiser is mainly the retailer or merchant; the network is the platform where the affiliate chooses the offer; the publisher is the affiliate who connects the consumer or the customer with the product that the consumer finally ends up buying. Affiliate marketing is a complex playing field that has only grown in complexity over the years.

With the increase in complexity, there was increase in the complexity of the role of the affiliate. This resulted in several levels of affiliate players, such as, super-affiliates, third party vendors and management firms.

Affiliate marketing overlaps with internet marketing strategies because some of the advertising strategies used by affiliate marketing such as Search Engine Optimization (SEO), content marketing, e-mail marketing and so on are also some of the common strategies used by internet marketing. Affiliate marketing also uses some uncommon methods of advertising such as review publication of the service or the product sold by their partners and used by the consumer.

Referral Marketing vs. Affiliate Marketing

People usually confuse affiliate marketing with referral marketing since they both have a common basis. Both of them use third parties to promote sales. However, both these marketing worlds are very distinct and different from each other. The starkest difference is that referral marketing uses a more personal, trust-based relationship to increase sales while affiliate marketing utilizes finance as a motivation to promote sales. Affiliate marketing usually has a lower profile when compared to the more conventional methods of attracting online vendors. Advertisers usually overlook affiliate marketing in preference for search engines and e-mail. However, affiliate still has a significant role in the e-commerce.

How it Started

William J. Tobin first introduced affiliate marketing to the world of e-commerce. Since its inception affiliate marketing has grown by leaps and bounds. Offline businesses were always an integral part of a business plan, but e-commerce websites and platforms soon become just as important to the overall business as the conventional offline business plans. Sectors such as retail industries, file sharing and adult gambling became the most dynamic sectors of affiliate marketing.

The late arrivals to the Internet, such as blogging and interactive online communities have helped in the growth of the communication links between affiliates and the retailers. There are a number of business platforms to enhance the communication between affiliates and retailers. Affiliate marketing is also popularly dubbed as "performance marketing" in reference to how it replaces sales employees. The advertisers don't usually employ affiliates; they are the extended arm of sales for the business they promote. Affiliate managers usually run outsourced program management companies that are used by retailers. This is similar to the role of the advertising agency server.

Why Affiliate Marketing is the Business for You

Let's have a look at some of the numerous reasons why you should be part of affiliate marketing.

Part time profession

Affiliate marketing is a business that can be run part time to give you a bit of extra income on the side. It is the very definition of passive income. It requires no expertise or degree. Just about anybody can join affiliate marketing and make a business out of it, be it a retiree who wants to add a little something to his pension or a student who is looking to make his or her way through college to pay off tuition loans. You just need to sign up with a company and allow them to advertise on your blog or website.

Minimal Office Needs

Since you don't require a physical office for this kind of marketing, you don't have a need for administration. You don't have to convince customers to sell your products. You don't have to worry about being able to pay your staff. Most importantly, you don't have to worry about customers returning orders. Your only concern is making sure that people who visit your blog or website click on the advertisements. This can easily be accomplished by ensuring that there is a relevance between the content on your blog or website and the advertisements that are shown.

Convenient

In the recent times, affiliate marketing has shifted entirely to the Internet. This makes it very convenient, not to mention profitable. It makes the job very flexible and you can now make any space your workplace. You can easily work on this without compromising on your daily life or your full-time job or any other commitments you might have. Being an online job, makes affiliate marketing a portable and global job. You can work from any part of the world as long as you can connect to the Internet. With the increase in the number of public spaces that have access to open and free Wi-Fi, you can even work during vacation or at the airport while you wait for your flight. You can keep track of your projects, connect with new affiliates and enjoy your life at the same time. Since there are no work timings or time limitations you don't have to worry about reaching office and working for a set number of hours a day and being productive all the time. You can work just a couple of hours a day or you could work 24 hours a day, depending on how much time you can invest in it. And just because you don't work doesn't mean that you stop earning because your website or blog is still functional and you will still earn.

Low Investment High Return

If you consider starting your own company based on affiliate marketing, it is obvious that your startup costs are very low. The overhead costs are also low. For a regular business you need to worry about a number of things, such as taking a loan, finding a space for your company, sales of your product and overhead costs. All this worry disappears when it comes to affiliate marketing. You don't need a lot of money to start an affiliate business. You don't have to worry about rent or staff payments.

This is similar to making money from billboards. Billboard owners pay building owners money to advertise. The income from this is far more than the costs you incur. There is no need to worry about continuous income flow because as long as the advertisement is on your building, you will get the money. Affiliate marketing is like this because for as long as the advertisement is on your website or blog you will get paid. To top it all, you are the sole owner and don't need to pay anything to run the business.

The amount of effort you need to put in is also less. You just need to add the links on your website or blog and wait for a visitor to click on it. Once a visitor clicks on it, you get paid. You physically don't do anything to sell the product besides adding the link to your website. You save time and effort that you can utilize for other things such as your daily job or other productive things. This is particularly useful for bloggers who can now focus on blogging without worrying about bills and payments in general.

Freedom to Choose

One of the main advantages of affiliate marketing is that you can choose your affiliate. You can choose which retailer you want to advertise. No company can force you to advertise their product. You can also advertise things that are related to your blog. For example, if your blog is about baking, you can advertise a well-known retailer for baking goods such as baking trays, decorations and so on. This opens up opportunities for your viewers. They can have a place to start with and use your blog as a way to guide them. You can also push certain products by recommending them, sharing testimonials about them or reviewing them. You have to make sure that you don't over sell the product.

Benefits of Affiliate Marketing

If a retailer goes through affiliate marketing, he can get a lot more customers just by placing advertisements on websites. This saves him time on promotions, which he can now use to do other useful things. The retailer will also get a much bigger platform, when compared to conventional advertising, to advertise his goods. This also means the retailer doesn't have to actually search for customers, instead the customers come to him.

Customer Data

Using the affiliate's website or blog, it's easy for the retailer to build a database of customers. This gives the retailer an analysis of the average behavior of customers. Startup websites can use affiliate marketing to find their foothold to run their own business. The financial profit or gain would also increase, as they don't have to invest much in this kind of marketing.

Beneficial to everyone

This type of marketing system benefits everybody. The retailer doesn't have to pay the affiliate until a visitor from his website becomes a customer. The business owner does not pay unless his product is sold or unless a specific minimum amount that is sold. It also benefits the customer because the website advertisement takes them not only to the product but also delivery of the product right at their doorstep. It saves them the time it would take for them to drive down to buy the product.

Optimization of advertising

Most people depend on search engines to filter out websites to buy products from. The affiliate can also make sure that the retailer is listed higher on the search engine. This increases the chances of customers going to the link and buying something from the retailer. This also increases the probability of the retailer selling a product. Another advantage of search engines is the fact that there is no downtime for the advertisement. Most affiliate websites have a membership scheme that allows them to customize the advertisements based on the customer membership and their search history. This creates knowledge about the customer, which the affiliate uses to show them specific products so as to ensure that they are satisfied with the products advertised to them. Most of the affiliate's website will have advertisements that target specific groups of people for a specific type of goods. This allows targeted sales and a better-optimized advertising plan.

Marketing is Covered

With affiliates in place, the retailer doesn't have to worry about marketing; he can focus his efforts on how to expand his business. The affiliate makes sure that the retailer shows up at the top of searches in search engines. The affiliate just increases the retailer's chance of being found in search engines by increasing the number of listings for the merchants. This is a useful thing for small business that is still trying to find a place in the world of e-commerce. This ensures that the customers are brought to the retailer rather than the retailer waiting for the customers to show up. The more customers who come to the retailer's website just drives up the demand of the retailer which further increases his sales. The real trick is to get the retailer into the top two pages of results on a search engine. This greatly improves the chances of customers finding the retailer.

Transparency in Operation

Another major advantage of affiliate marketing is the transparency with which it operates. This increases trust between all the parties involved. The sales are transparent and can easily be tracked to ensure that there is no discrepancy in sales. Most retailer run their business with minimal investment since it is the fastest way to start a home run company. There is no risk involved with affiliate marketing, as there are no limitations in how much you earn. You can also track the number of products sold. There will also be a live count of the number of people who visit through the retailer's website.

You are your own boss

Affiliate marketing does not involve a lot of investment in terms of infrastructure or administration. This makes you your own boss since you do not have to report to anybody. You can work how much ever you want, where you want to and when you want to. You can operate on your own timings. You can fix timings to deal with retailers or customers as to your convenience. You can also choose which retailers you want to promote and advertise depending on your interest. This ensures that you give your complete focus to your job and don't resent it. Another major advantage is that you can work from where ever you want. If your day job takes to another city, you can easily shift your business without worrying about workspace or employees or any other hassle that conventional company owners face. You will never lose your clients since your business is entirely online. This also means that your clientele is only limited to the people you can reach and not where your company is set up. You will always find clients no matter where you go.

No need to worry about paid leave

You don't have to worry about taking leave from your online business because you can earn even on vacation. All you need is a computer and a Wi-Fi connection. Traveling also gives you insights into the culture of the various places you visit and you can try to include these insights in your advertising. You can relax and expand your business at the same time. In a corporate job, you will always need to worry about running out of money at the end of the month but when you take up affiliate marketing you won't have to worry about running out of money. There will be a constant cash flow as long as you advertise retailers. It also gives you the scope to expand and hone your skills. A corporate job often stifles your development in the field because of the person ranked above you be it a co-worker or your boss. In affiliate marketing, you are your own boss so you can develop as much as you want and still have time to relax.

If you plan to make affiliate marketing a full-time job, you can always take breaks as you wish or vacations when you want because you can always carry your job with you. There is no specific location or office that you need to work from, so you can always work from anywhere in the world and still make it work. You can pursue any hobby that you have always wanted to do and manage your affiliate marketing business on the side. It allows you to live your life to the fullest. If you only want to do affiliate marketing as a part time business you can still use it as an opportunity to try new things and hone skills.

Chapter 5:

Using Search Engines to your Advantage

Once your website is all set up, the first thing you need to do is to market yourself. Having a creative and attractive website will get you nowhere if you do not market it properly. You need to create a plan on how you plan to advertise a website. There are a large number of perfect websites that offer a number of products and services to essentially the same type of clients. The trick will be to make your visible and noticeable amongst all these websites. This is particularly hard because of the dominance of the big names in the field such as Google or Bing. When a potential customer needs to buy a product, or needs a service, they usually turn to these big names instead of looking at the solution you might have. The aesthetics of your website might decide the ranking of your website but the number of customers is always decided by the way you market it. If you don't advertise your website, the only way people will find your website is by looking up the specific name or the URL. The chances of you finding customers this way is very slim.

Online advertising gets very easy when you register with a major search engine. This will help you reach out and get the attention of the people you plan to target. If the search engine you register with already has a good number of followers, then it will be even easier for you to get customers. When a potential customer looks up a product related to your website then your website automatically shows up in the results page. You've now got yourself a new customer. It might also be a wise decision to go for the search engine that expects you to pay for their services. You might have to shell out some money but it'll be worth it because you will get some assurance that your website is actually reaching people. If you go with free search engines, then you most likely end up in a spam list and you never know if your website gets any advertisement. Paid search engines give your website top priority. There are even some search engines that allow you to pay according to the number of customers you get through their search engines.

Once you register your website under a search engine, you will need to follow it up by tracing your site in the search engine. You should keep track of where your website pops up on the results page when a search is done using specific key words. If your website appears too low on the results, then you should probably consider other forms of advertising or rethinking your advertising strategy. Most people do not go beyond the second page of results when they are trying to find a product or service. So, if your website is beyond the second page then there is the chance that it is not reaching anybody. You need to then work on improving the rank of your website.

To improve your site using search engines, you need to follow a couple of tips. You could also hire a consultant who can help improve your site and develop it. However, if you are just starting your business this might be difficult since you might not have enough cash inflow to invest in hiring a professional. If you do have the money to invest in perfecting your advertising through search engines, then do not hesitate to spend it. Every cent will be worth it. Most startups or even street vendors have websites advertising their business because it is the smartest way to get out there in the market. You do not need to invest in an office space. You can run your business from the comfort of your home. Using the tips mentioned below you can easily improve your website without spending a lot of money.

Using catchy names and titles

Give your domain a bit of flair. The theme of your website and your business should be the major factors involved in deciding your domain name. It needs to be relevant to your business and also has to catch the viewer's eye. Keep it simple. A simple and catchy name will make it easy for the customers to remember the website. Make sure you register with the top search engines such as Google, MSN, Bing, Yahoo and Ask. These search engines might be more expensive but most people prefer to use one of these search engines.

Networking

You might have this impression that since your business is now online you do not need to network or focus on building up connections. This is not entirely true. Networking always help. It is key to promoting your business. If you want to expand your business you need to connect with people and learn from them. It will help spread the word about your website and succeed in bringing in more customers. You can initially start by spreading information of your domain to other websites by sharing your link to them. In return, you can add their site links on your website or promote them in some way.

Pay per Click

Pay per click is the trending way to advertise one's website or business. Most websites with a high ranking have built their websites using this mode of advertising. The basis for this mode of advertising is that you can use better ranked websites to advertise your site by paying them every time somebody clicks on your link through their website. This was you pay only when you get a customer and don't have to constantly pay the website owner even when you aren't getting customers from their site. This will allow you to direct customers from other websites to your websites. This is even more useful when you advertise on websites relevant to your business or website.

Formatting Advertisements

Formats for advertisements differ from search engine to search engine. So, it is essential that you know the format for the advertisements before you create one and set it up. Read up on the different format of advertising for different search engines and pick ones that are most suited to you or ones you feel are within your grasp of advertising. However, there are some basic strategies to formatting an advertisement:

- The heading of the advertisement should focus on what you want to sell or provide to the customer. You have a limited number of characters to sell your business, so it's up to you to catch the customer with your heading. If you just use that space to give the name of your business, then you will just be wasting precious space. You can use the heading space to give some important information about your product or service.

- Follow proper formats and ensure you make the advertisement aesthetically appealing. If you use too many capitals, your customer might just get intimidated and not bother in looking through your website. It is also unprofessional and you will lose your standing in the market.

- Keep abbreviations to a minimum because you can never assume that all your viewers know what the abbreviation stands for. They might misunderstand it and expect something or just ignore your website because they can't understand the abbreviations. There are high chances of people knowing the popular abbreviations but it would be better to avoid abbreviations as much as possible.

Usage of Key Words

One of the most important things in online advertising is figuring out what key words or target words would help in customers reaching your website or vice versa. Keep updating the key words you use so that you can connect your customers to your website.

Mobile Compatibility

In the age of mobile phones, making your phone compatible for phones is essential. Most people no longer have time to look at websites only from their laptops. They tend to shop on the go, from their mobile phones. So, make sure website supports both phones and laptops.

Connect to Customers

Keeping in touch with your customers is integral. You can do this by utilizing online applications or by allowing your customers to review your service and website. Nowadays people look for websites that are highly ranked and recommended by fellow people before buying something. Providing a mail ID or local address and other information makes it easy for people from your region or regions close to you to contact you. Even if you have international clients, it is always better to have some local clients as well. You should also claim your Google local page to get some visibility and establish a name for yourself in your locality. You can also provide details such as the timings within which you operate, phone number, email ID and so on.

Besides making use of advertisements to promote your business, affiliate marketing is to also help you make some money. So, you should also be careful when you are advertising other websites on your website. Be wary of the cheats. Also, make sure that you put up advertisements that are relevant to your business.

Myths on Affiliate Marketing

Affiliate marketing has a number of myths that surround it mainly due to the good and easy money that is involved. Most people hesitate from getting into affiliate marketing mainly because of the myths that surround the field. Here are some of the myths that surround affiliate marketing:

Affiliate Marketing is a Scam

One of the most frequent myths of affiliate marketing is that it is not easy to get into affiliate marketing. Affiliate marketing is a job that will fetch you money if you have a clear idea about what you want to do. You just need to know what you should do and how you need to do it.

Affiliate Marketing Doesn't Require Much Management

The bottom line is that it takes some work to create and maintain a website well enough to make money. It is always possible to create a website but it takes some skill to keep it going. The content of the website needs to be constantly updated and in tune with current trends.

Affiliate Marketing does not care about Consumers

Another famous myth about affiliates is that consumers do not agree or like affiliate marketing. Ten years ago, people might not have believed the existence of affiliate marketing but now they are just fine with affiliate marketing. People will be attracted to your website if you are creative and promote your business well.

Affiliate Marketing is not easy

Most people believe that affiliate marketing is too tough. However, the essential thing is that if they spend time on it, they can see that it is one of the easiest ways to start and promote a business. When they gather all the information they need and then sit down to start affiliate marketing then it would be very easy. With time and dedication, you can get nearly anywhere.

Chapter 6:

Importance of Passive Income

The way most people work today is on an active-income credo basis. They get paid according to the quantity, quality and/or nature of services they provide to a firm. What they receive as compensation is what we call the person's active income. They keep getting it as long as they are working.

Now let's assume, for a minute, that the person fails to provide their services to the firm in the future for some unforeseen reason – maybe they got into a bad accident and couldn't work for a year – what happens then? Their one and only source of income gets disrupted and they have no way to sustain themselves except for any savings they might have. This is problematic for a number of reasons, not the least of which is reducing job security in the service sector with the ever-increasing competition.

You see, every market works on the principle of supply and demand, and in the human resource market, the supply is almost always higher than the demand, i.e. the number of people willing to offer their services for a particular compensation is always higher than the number of people required for that particular service. This means that anyone can be replaced at any time. Lay-offs happen all the time, and it's a difficult time for the employees when they do happen. So in case an individual happens to lose their job, it's always advantageous to have a secondary source of income. This is why I recommend having a source of passive income so much. Depending solely on your active income source is completely stupid and risky.

Passive income usually requires little to no active effort on your part, and it is a source of continuous income, so it is totally fine for an individual to have both an active and a passive source of income at a given time. If you so wish to, you can always redirect your passive income to a retirement fund. A better idea, however, is to invest it into an enterprise which you are really passionate about and believe to have a high chance of success. In this way, you will not affect your regular lifestyle or expenditure capacity, but you will still be able to become richer over time. You can – and I recommend you should – also save part of your passive income to contribute towards a fund for any future uncertainties.

Passive Income

Now, the next thing I want you to think very carefully about is your time. Time is the most valuable resource you have, and you need to prioritize your actions effectively so that you make the best use of your abilities and finish by being as productive as you can at the end of the day. This is very crucial if you want to make smart use of your wealth. You absolutely *need* to separate your time from the money you earn.

Next, forget that multitasking is a thing. It isn't, not when it comes to investing your time and efforts efficiently. You can't invest them in different avenues at the same time, so it's best to focus on one thing at a time. For this, you have to pick an enterprise that doesn't need regular involvement and effort from you but still manages to generate regular income for you. This makes you much more efficient since by just inventing a small sum of money, you are securing a constant flow of income to your account. This allows you to direct your real skills towards job that require active effort on your part for you to be able to earn.

The greatest joy of having a source of passive income is that it is independent of your level of involvement for the most part, unlike your regular income source. Most active income sources give you the income directly proportional to your investment of time, effort, and other resources. With passive income, that is not the case. You only have to set it up once and then you can leave it to its own devices. Yes, you can increase its longevity and efficiency by investing more money and time, but in the end, that's totally your choice and it's not really a necessity. If you wish to, you can invest further into it, and if you don't want to, you may as well not. It is in the nature of passive income that you only need to put in some effort and money at the initial stages. After that, it will continue to generate wealth for you over time. This is why it is such a promising way of dealing with future uncertainties that you and your family might have to face at some point.

So if you wish to have a healthy financial state and want to grow your wealth constantly, it is of utmost importance for you to start thinking about creating a source of passive income and then making some efforts towards actually achieving this. Let's take a closer look at this and see why having a passive income is so important. This will motivate you to stop wasting your time and start acting in the right direction at the earliest. Don't deliberate; *act*!

Liberty

One thing we all have in common, regardless of where we're born, how we've been raised, what we've studied, how much we're earning, or what we're doing with our lives, is that we all get only twenty four hours every day. You can save your money, your assets, and almost anything else for future use, but the one thing that you can't save for future use, no matter how rich or powerful you are, is time. Time keeps flowing, and it waits for nobody. It doesn't discriminate on the basis of status, ability, caste, or anything else. It just does its own thing. And this is what brings out the difference between the rich, successful people and the not-so-rich, unsuccessful people. The successful people value time more than anything else, and they make the best use of it, whereas the unsuccessful fail to do so.

In a person's life, the inflow-outflow of cash and commodities is a very regular thing and it keeps happening as long as he lives. Money changes hands and property is bought and sold all the time. The only thing that *can't be* bought or sold is time. Once a moment has passed, you don't get it back, ever. This is what makes time the most important resource in our lives. The possibilities of what we can do with our time are endless, so it is up to us to decide how we want to invest our time. We should be thinking about the activity that gives us the best returns on our investment of time.

This is why making your income and your time mutually exclusive is very vital. When you're under monetary constraints, trying to meet your monthly expenditures all the time, you are always busy. But when you are not struggling to make ends meet that is when you can truly shine and channelize your creativity and energy into doing something really rewarding. You can take up a hobby or an old interest of yours. You can even try and find new hobbies. My father is one of the best examples of this. After having built a multi-million dollar business, he settled into an easy lifestyle in his fifties and started enjoying life to it's fullest. In my growing years, he would always tell me how much he had wanted to learn music in his youth. Well, he got his wish, albeit much later in his life. But hey, he still really enjoyed it. He learned to sing and play a few of his favorite instruments really well. You can also be that guy if you create a good source of passive income for yourself.

Most people feel completely consumed by their obligations towards their families that all they ever do is try to make ends meet and fulfill their monthly financial responsibilities. Work doesn't bring them any joy at that point, as it only becomes a means for survival. With each passing day, they start to loathe their jobs more and more, because they have no time for recreation. They are not able to pursue any of their interests, and this leads to unrest and misery. They can't experiment, they can't be spontaneous, and they can't be adventurous. It takes the joy out of life, honestly. And I say that is no way to lie. You don't want a stagnant life, do you? You want the freedom to be able to try new things without the fear of failure holding you back.

Passive income gives you that. It doesn't suddenly free you from all your daily obligations, but it sure frees you from the plight of living paycheck to paycheck. You just have more free time and resources to harness your potential, experiment, and not feel constrained by you daily obligations, financial or otherwise.

Having a steady source of passive income gives you the wings you've always wanted. It lets you put your creative energies to wherever you want them to go, and opens up a world of whole new possibilities for you to explore that you never could before. At first, your passive income may not even be close to your monthly expenses, but over time, it will grow, and reach a break-even point eventually. When this happens, you will be able to survive completely on your passive income, and this is when you will truly have the keys to the Lamborghini, the opportunity you need to start living your life the way you truly want to. You will be the master of your time and you will no longer be bound by your old routine.

So to sum it all up, having a good source of steady passive income gives you the freedom to invest your time and money wherever you wish to with full liberty. You will have a much better financial stability and you will discover yourself in new ways because you will not be bound by any constraints. This can never happen when you're living paycheck to paycheck.

A Secure Future

Most of us want stability in our lives at some point or the other. Even if you're a really adventurous lad in your twenties and maybe even early thirties, during the later stages of your life, you just have to tone down the spontaneity a little bit and start thinking about some stability. This is because you're growing old and you are not sure of what the future holds. It's critically important for you to think about your future and find ways to secure it for yourself and your family so you don't find yourself stuck into unforeseen troubles.

Like I mentioned before, someone who earns their livelihood by working on a day-to-day basis, rendering services in exchange of remuneration, is at a lot of risk. Let's take the example of a construction worker. For someone like that, their hands are the most important part of their body, since their hands are what helps him or her earn their livelihood, right? Now think about what would happen if the worker were to suddenly lose both his hands in an unfortunate accident? All of a sudden, his one and only source of income will disappear. He won't have any money to feed himself or his family. This is a devastating situation, and one must try to find ways to avoid such scenarios at all costs. This is where passive income acts as your safeguard. It secures your and your family's well being in case of any untoward happenings, and this puts your mind at ease.

This is even more useful for people who work in an industry that's constantly under flux. If there is a lot of corporate downsizing going on all the time, then it's best to have a good source of passive income. That way, you don't need to fixate on your problem of job insecurity, and hence, financial instability. You can meet your monthly expenses easily and maintain your normal lifestyle without making any compromises. This also gives you a sense of calm and confidence, which is an added bonus.

Follow your Dreams

Most of us don't have the luxury of following our dreams and pursuing our passions because we just don't have the time to invest in those things. Try to remember the last time you took your car out on a leisurely drive and not just to reach your office. If you don't recall it, you probably belong in the category of people mentioned above. We're all so indulged in the act of trying to earn our daily bread that we've forgotten to enjoy life. The tertiary sector is all-encompassing now, and a lot of people are earning their livelihood through it, giving up everything in order to barely survive. It's a tough world out there. Primary sector is shrinking, and so is people's will to follow their passions. This is where the passive income comes in to save the day. When you have a steady flow of passive income flowing in, you have better control over your life and your time, so you can afford to spend it on your interests and passions.

Like we've talked about in one of the previous chapters, you need to separate your time from your work, and once you do that, you will have plenty of it to do what pleases you. Want to take a family vacation to Bahamas? Sure. Feel like painting? Go right ahead. Maybe you want to build a motorcycle. I say, why the hell not? When you are not burdened with the pressure of earning your daily bread through a nine to five job, you will have a lot of opportunities to follow your heart. If your passive income takes care of your debts and prior commitments, can you imagine how cool would that be? You won't have to wait for your paycheck every month. You will engage in more rewarding and satisfying jobs with relative ease.

We all know that we're more productive when we're doing something we actually enjoy. On the other hand, when we're working to only earn money, our work is suboptimal at best. This notion should be completely done away with, in my opinion. When you're not thinking about work twenty-four - seven, you can actually invest time in grooming your personality and self-development. All you need to do is devote some time, and you will have that once you have a steady passive income flowing in. Maybe you used to like playing the guitar back in college but now it's eating dust sitting in one corner of your house. Maybe you used to love painting and were even quite good at it in your younger days. Well, now is as good a time as any to pick those things up and get practicing again. When you're financially secure, you will have both the time and the motivation to start following your passions.

Freedom of Movement

I absolutely love travelling, and my guess is that you do to. Most people love travelling and exploring new places they've never been to. It carries a thrill that you can't find in anything else. But for most people, it isn't possible to travel even half as often as they would like to. This is because of professional commitments they have that hinder them from taking out time to travel. But if you spend most of your life stuck in a building, it can be pretty boring. To be really able to enjoy life, you need some freedom of movement. This is possible with passive income, because when you have a steady flow of income without any effort, you have time and money to spare. You can use them to travel wherever you want to.

And hey, this is not just about traveling for leisure either. In case if you have trouble at your job, or say you have been laid off in a mass lay off from your firm, you can easily move to a different place and start working there because your passive income provides you the security to do that. You have a financial cushion that lets you stay safe and plan your course of action in the future much better. Because of this cushion, you don't panic and make haphazard decisions that you might regret later.

When you think about it, for most of us, vacation is a welcome change because it provides us with a chance to enjoy, which is lacking in the daily monotony of life. It is nothing but a few ephemeral seconds of bliss pushed between the hard realities of our daily lives. But with a good source of steady passive income, you don't have to live your life that way anymore. You don't have to worry about depleting your cash reserves and you can live your whole life as a vacation, in a sense. You get the freedom of space and movement and the constraints that have been holding you back from travelling and moving around keep disappearing with time.

Once you've done that little bit of investment of time and resources in the beginning, you are no longer hindered by your scheduled and your day-job-dependent lifestyle. And this is good news for those people, too, who have always wanted to switch professions but they haven't been able to so far because of financial insecurities. This way, they can venture out into the world of opportunities again and do what they want to do. If you want movement in your life, passive income is absolutely crucial for you.

Chapter 7:

Different Niches To Make Money

As explained in the previous chapters, Affiliate marketing refers to tying up with third party companies in order to promote their products and services. This is a unique way to earn an income and also one of the easiest. But it will be important to have a large audience base, as that is the only way to avail good affiliates. Once you tie up with the third party, you will sprinkle the links to their products and services all over your website or blog. You will make money from it every time someone clicks on the link.

Hence, what is the best Niche to make money as an affiliate? Niche markets refer to those that are well established. Unfortunately, or perhaps, fortunately, there are quite a few of them when it comes to earning a passive income. The explanation is quite straightforward. Basically, any niche that has tons of customers and quality affiliate products to offer can be profitable in the long haul, provided you take a smart and systematic business-like approach to your affiliate marketing activity.

Finding a niche is one of the most daunting steps in an affiliate marketer's journey. But it's a step that can't be overlooked or rushed through. That being said, I have classified various niches and recommended other passive income strategies which can help you identify your interests and strength that you can compete in.

Making Money Online

The online industry is booming and one of the most popular sources to avail passive income. From YouTube to blogs, there are many ways to earn a handsome parallel income on a monthly basis. Here is looking at some of the different options available.

Websites/ blogs

Websites and blogs remain one of the most popular and high yielding online domains for passive income. Right from healthcare to beauty to cooking and sports, there are a plethora of options to pick from.

Starting a website is now quite easy. Just a few steps are required to set it up and you will be all set to host the website. Websites make for some of the best ways to connect to a large audience and is also quite easy to manage the outcome. The challenge will be to remain unique and provide them with never before seen content. It pays to do some research and come up with a winning strategy.

Blogs are just as easy and effective to pursue. If you have a flair for writing interesting content sure to capture the imagination of your audience, then start blogging to earn a passive income. It is easier to manage as compared to websites as you do not have to do too much towards its upkeep, apart from posting new content every now and then. It is possible to make anywhere about $100 to $1000 per week, through blogging, based on the type of content you provide your audience.

Estores

Estores are a great source to earn an online passive income. Estores are a lot easier to set up as compared to physical stores. You will be required to set up a website and start selling your products. Linking it to your social media accounts will help you kickstart the selling process as more and more people will know of your store's presence.

You can have your own store or sell on a site like amazon or eBay. The advantage with the latter is that you won't have to do too much towards the setup of the website. Sign up to become a seller and the website will take care of the rest.

Buy your products in bulk from websites like alibaba.com in order to avail a good discount and sell them on the third-party sites. It will pay to be aware of the latest trends in order to make the most of it. This type of business is slowly becoming one of the most preferred domains and sure to help you avail great profits.

Shipping

There is also the option to focus on the shipping aspect alone, if you do not wish to start an entire store. It calls for tying up with the websites in order to provide shipping. It is easy and makes for a great moneymaker. There are hundreds of websites to tie up with and can be picked based on whatever is convenient for you.

Training

Providing training is another niche market to pursue. From software training to skill development, there are many ways to capture an audience. Hosting private tutorials and online workshops is a great way to make a passive income. It is also quite easy, as you do not have to leave the comfort of your home. All you have to do is advertise about it in order to inform people about the tutorials. Having a dedicated website will help you manage your audience. Set up the classes as per your convenience.

Translation

The translation business is now booming owing to globalization. Right from translating books to information to other such data, there are many people looking for their content to be translated into regional languages. If you are good at one such language, then it will be a great opportunity for you to capitalize upon it. Choose to translate books, research findings etc. and other such information that you are comfortable with. You will have the chance to work on it during your spare time thereby making for a good option.

Comparison site

Comparison sites are now extremely popular. They compare prices of the same product and pick the lowest price for the customer. It is low maintenance and makes for a great passive income resource.

Freelancing

Freelancing is now easier than ever. It involves working with numerous clients and setting your own work timings. There is no traditional office set up and you have the option to work from anywhere you like. It is quite unconventional but makes for a great way to earn a passive income.

Right from writing to singing to providing information on the latest technologies, there are many options for a freelancer to pick from. Sites such as freelancer and Fiverr make for a great place to find and manage your clients. Freelancing is open to all and can make for a great option to earn a sustained passive income.

Ebooks

Ebooks are now extremely popular owing to the utility that they provide. With more and more people switching over to the online platform to read books and avail information, it is that much easier to pursue this domain. There are hundreds of topics to choose from and can publish as many different books as you like. Health and beauty are some of the best topics to choose from, as there are many takers for it. There are many websites to sell your books on that cater to the ebook format. Choose the one that suits you best.

Product Reviews

YouTube is a great platform to pursue in order to avail a passive income. One of the most popular videos on the site is product reviews. These reviews can range from everyday products such as kitchen appliances to beauty products such as cosmetics.

All you are required to do is pick up a product and review it for your audience and rate it at the end. A good idea is to announce when you will be posting a new video so that people are prepared for it and will be sure to check it out.

Google operates YouTube, so you will have to sign up with them. Based on the popularity of your videos, they will automatically start playing ads. When someone clicks on the ad, they are redirected to the website. You will have to make a minimum of $100 in order to have the money transferred to your account. It is generally paid by the 15th of the month but can be availed at a later date.

Competition

Remember that the only way to survive in this niche market is by producing good quality work. There will be stiff competition from a wide range of people including established bloggers, YouTubers, celebrities and athletes all promoting their products and channels. You must put in efforts and come up with good quality information that is unique and well researched.

Health (Weight Loss)

Health is wealth and important for everyone to maintain an ideal weight. But stress, junk foods and bad lifestyle choices all contribute towards weight gain making it difficult for a person to remain healthy. That makes way for the weight loss industry to flourish, as it proves to be lucrative market for weight loss products and advice.

Here is looking at how to make a mark in the industry.

Books/ Ebooks

Consider writing books on the topic. People tend to rely on advice gained through books, and invest far more trust than what they hear or see on the television. It will, therefore, make for a good choice to pursue. Ebooks are one of the most popular forms of media on the Internet. It is more beneficial to write ebooks as compared to hard copies.

There is no limit to the topics to pick from. From diets such as Paleo, to exercise routines such as CrossFit, there are many different options available.

There are many places to sell your ebooks. Amazon is the leading portal for ebooks and you will find it easy to sell on it. They will also have a user-friendly publishing website, which makes it easier for you to publish and sell the books. This market can be welcoming to both beginners and established writers. But research is a must, owing to the stiff competition. As per studies, one of the best niche markets is focusing on women's healthcare. Women are most concerned with their health and catering to their needs will make for a great entry platform into this line of business.

Consider employing freelancers for the job. They will know the tricks of the trade and turn over a book that can give you a competitive edge. Revising the book from time to time and incorporating the latest information can help to sell the book better.

DVDS / Videos

DVDs are still quite popular and make for a great way to enter the healthcare domain. It is easier to practically show people what they can do in order to enhance their health. Right from showing the different physical exercises to guiding them through the nutritional aspect, it will be easier to cater to a larger audience. However, it will be important to present it in a unique way and ensure that it makes people get on their feet and start following the exercises. Yoga is one of the best-selling DVDs. It appeals to a wide audience and keep you in the loop. Choose to carry out the positions yourself or employ a professional for the task.

YouTube

If you are not keen on making a DVD then YouTube makes for a good choice. You will have the chance to make and share videos that cater to a wide audience. YouTube has now massively grown in popularity and is one of the most frequented websites in the world. Make and share videos with ease and more importantly, keep in touch with your audiences. It is quite easy to start a channel and start posting the videos. Based on the popularity, you will make money based on the number of clicks that your video gets. It will be important to make it as interesting as possible in order to capture and maintain the audience.

Websites

The healthcare industry is now booming and one of the best niche markets on the Internet. Online healthcare consulting is a great domain to explore, owing to the number of people seeking help. From discussing health issues to providing online advice, there are many options to choose from. Providing nutritional advice is now a big market. Seems like every other person I meet is trying to lose weight and develop a healthy body. This makes it a great platform to reach out to a vast number of people in need of nutritional advice. Setting up a website dedicated to providing such advice will make for a great way to capitalize on the popularity of the domain.

Fitness studio

Opening a fitness studio is also a great idea. As mentioned, with more and more people looking to lose weight and develop a lean body, it will be a great idea to start a health-based studio. There are many fields to focus on including yoga, Pilates and aerobics.

A small place will also work, as you can always teach people in batches. You might have to undertake a course in order to earn a certificate. Once done, advertise about the classes in local media and Facebook, which will help you receive new clients. If the business is a hit, then consider employing more people to work under you.

Romance

Another great domain to pursue is dating and romance. There seems to be a burst in the number of people breaking the shackles of traditional ways to meet new people. This makes for a great opportunity for people to capitalize on the trend.

The following are the two best ways to make the most of this trend.

Websites

Starting a romance or love based website makes for a good choice. You will be able to provide relationship advice to your audience members. Hosting fun games will help you keep your audience entertained and keep them coming back for more. The website can also make for a meeting platform for people looking for love. A matrimonial site will make for a good option, as it will be easier to manage the content.

Ebooks

Ebooks in the romance fiction genre sell like hot cakes and are extremely popular among young adults. Even romance and relationship advice based non-fiction books are in demand in the market.

Apps

Dating apps are now extremely popular all over the world. From helping two people meet to suggesting great pick up lines, there are a whole host of options to pursue. Dating sites are easy to build and will make for extremely lucrative options. Try to introduce a unique element so that people pick your app over the others. Keep up with the times and ensure that you provide your audience with interesting content.

Beauty on Wheels

The beauty business is fast growing and provides for a great opportunity to earn a passive income.

Providing at-home salon services is the latest trend in the world of beauty. If you are trained in grooming, then visit the clients at their homes in order to provide the chosen beauty services. This is a good way to invest in the business, as you will have the freedom to provide the service according to your convenience.

Apart from beauty services, you also have the option to provide massage therapy, manicures, etc. Reflexology is now quite popular and will make for a great platform to pursue.

Pet grooming is another booming industry. With more and more people wanting to have their pets rock the latest styles, it makes for a great platform to avail passive income. Take up a training process and start your pet-grooming salon.

Apps and Testing

App building and testing is a good option for those in the technology field. Apps can be built during spare time and released on PlayStore, the Appstore and Windows in order to earn an income. There are many options to pick from ranging from games to beauty apps to food delivery apps, with thousands of users readily available to download new products.

Testing refers to testing out software and apps. It is important, as the end product should be usable and convenient for the end user. So, more and more companies employ people to test out their apps before releasing it to the audiences. It makes for a simple job that pays quite well. If you are already adept at it then it will be very easy for you to work on it to avail a passive income.

Stocks and Real Estate

The stock market is booming and provides a great opportunity to capitalize upon. It makes for a great source of passive income, as there is a lot of potential for both beginners and experienced hands. Stocks are easy to buy and sell, especially penny stocks. But you will have to do a little research before getting started with it in order to make the most of it.

If you are not confident enough in investing yourself then hire a broker to get you started. Once you get the hang of it, you will be able to start trading by yourself. It takes just a little effort to have the software setup. Once done, start buying and selling the stocks based on your research. Apart from stocks, there are many other types of financial instruments to pursue. Some of them include etf's, bonds and precious metals. Build your portfolio by picking instruments that are diverse in nature as that will cut down on your risk. In addition, you could always share some of your trading strategies or screenshots of your trading income on your website/blog to gain traffic. After all, that's what affiliate marketing is about.

Real estate is also a great option for those looking to earn a good passive income. Buying and renting a house will help you remain with a substantial profit. You will not need a big house or bungalow for it and just a small place will do the trick.

But care must be taken to pick a place that will grow in value over time. Upkeep of the property will also be your responsibility, so you must be prepared that, as well.

Passive Income

There is no limit to the number of passive income avenues to pursue, however, it will be important to limit it in number so as to be able to dedicate more time and effort to them.

Conclusion

We've reached the end of this book and I'm pleased to inform you that now you're equipped with all the information you need to go out and build yourself a great new business. Gradually, you will start to see a steady flow of passive income and it will likely increase over time. We've covered a lot of topics in this book so make sure you take your time with everything and do your own research to dig deeper into every topic. It's time for you to go out and take control of your finances. That's the only way to success, and now you're prepared for it.

I would like to thank you one last time for picking this book. It was a great experience to share all this knowledge with you and I hope you enjoyed reading it as much as I enjoyed writing it. Set your goals, and get down to work. Always stay humble and genuine.

Made in the USA
Middletown, DE
14 July 2022

69355692R00046